Christmas
AT STATION 17

Dan King

Art by Daniele Fabbri

Dedication

The holidays in the Fire Service are filled with love, service, and family. In the Fire Service, we have our family at home and we have our family at work. I want to recognize all of those that are in the Emergency Services that sacrifice daily and during the Holidays Season. During the holidays, First Responders are on duty and ready to protect our communities. I want to thank all First Responders: Firefighters, Police Officers, 911 Dispatchers, EMT's, Paramedics, and our Military who have chosen a career to protect and serve.

This book is dedicated to our future firefighters that will get to enjoy the Christmas Season at the Fire House and to the Fallen Firefighters and their families who made the ultimate sacrifice protecting our communities.

This is a work of fiction. Names, characters, places, and incidents either are the product of the author's imagination or are used fictitiously.

Copyright © 2024 by Dan King

All rights reserved. No part of this book may be reproduced or used in any manner without written permission of the copyright owner except for the use of quotations in a book review. For more information, contact: danking120@aol.com

First paperback edition November 2024

Book design by Veronica Scott
Illustrations by Daniele Fabbri

ISBN: 978-1-7368886-5-0 (Hardcover)

It's Christmastime, and Station 17 is all aglow with colorful lights twinkling through the snow. Inside, the firefighters are gearing up for a very merry and busy month.

A boy enters the station with his parents and sister. He pulls a wagon full of new toys.

"May I help you?" Chief Martinez asks.

"My name is Lincoln, and I have donations for the toy drive," the boy says. "I bought some of the toys with my own money."

"Thank you so much!" says Chief Martinez.

He leads Lincoln, his sister and his parents to a large toy-collection bin in the corner.

"Looks like we will need to make more room soon!" he says.

Chief Martinez walks the family outside.

"What do you think of our lights?" he asks.
"Do you think we will win the fire station decorating contest?"

"Yes!" Lincoln says, gazing at the sea of color before him.

"The prize is $1,000," says Chief Martinez. "If we win, we will donate the money to the animal shelter. If another fire station wins, they'll donate it to a charity they choose."

"I sure hope you win," Lincoln says.

"And I hope you are home on Sunday afternoon," Chief Martinez says. "If you hear sirens, come outside!"

"Why?" asks Lincoln.

"Because Station 17 will have a very special visitor from the North Pole. And he has asked us to drive him past the houses of all the kids who have been good this year."

That Sunday, Lincoln stares out the window.

"Mom, I don't hear sirens!" he says, his voice full of worry. "Was I not a good boy this year?"

His mother smiles. "Lincoln, that's impossible. You have been *very* good this year. In fact—"

But she gets cut off by the wail of a siren. Lincoln gasps and jumps off the couch. He pulls on his coat and boots and runs outside.

The siren gets louder and louder until Engine 19, all shiny and red, turns the corner. A figure stands on top of the truck.

"Santa!" Lincoln yells with glee.

"Ho ho ho!" Santa Claus bellows. He waves to Lincoln as Engine 19 passes.

The driver—Chief Martinez—honks the fire engine's horn. Its tone is even deeper than Santa's jolly voice.

Lincoln stares down the street even after the truck rolls out of sight. He stands there until the last strains of the siren fade in the distance.

The next weekend, Lincoln is Christmas shopping on Main Street with his parents and sister.

They are waiting to cross the street when Engine 19 rolls up.

"Hi, Chief Martinez!" says Lincoln brightly. "Are you going to a fire?'

"No, we would have our sirens on if we were. Today we are on our way to deliver all the toys we collected in the toy drive!"

"Cool!" Lincoln says. "Where are you bringing them?"

"First, we are going to the children's hospital to give toys to the sick kids. Then we are going to the church to give the rest to children in need."

Another week passes. Lincoln is back on Main Street with his mom and dad. But this time they are surrounded by many other families, with many other excited boys and girls. It's the day of the town's holiday parade!

A smiling man walks over. He is with a woman and a dark-haired boy.

The man looks familiar to Lincoln, but Lincoln can't place him.

'Hello, Lincoln!"
the man says.

"I get that a lot," Chief Martinez says, winking. Then he introduces Lincoln, his sister and his parents to his wife and son, Sam.

"I'm so excited for the parade!" Sam says. "Engine 19 will be in it, and Dad's firefighter friends are tossing out candy canes!"

Lincoln looks up at Chief Martinez. "If Engine 19 is in the parade, why aren't *you* in it?"

"Because it's my day off!" says Chief Martinez. "At Station 17 we work 24-hour shifts. In between, we get two days off. Since I don't work today, I get to enjoy the parade with my family—just like you!"

"That's cool!" says Lincoln . "And are you having Christmas Eve dinner at your house tomorrow, just like me?"

"Even cooler," says Sam. "We're having dinner at the firehouse!"

"At the firehouse?" asks Lincoln . "Why?"

"Well, my 24-hour shift starts tomorrow morning," Chief Martinez replies.

"You have to work on *Christmas Eve*?" Lincoln exclaims. "Why?"

"Because fires and emergencies don't stop just because it's a holiday," explains Chief Martinez. "We need firefighters ready at all times, just in case. And this year, it's my turn to be on duty on Christmas Eve."

Chief Martinez explains that each year, all the families of the firefighters on duty gather at the firehouse for Christmas Eve dinner. The firefighters cook some of the food in Station 17's kitchen. Their families bring the rest.

After dinner, they listen to Christmas music while the kids play. Each child gets a special Christmas present from the fire captain.

When it gets late, the families go home to sleep and wait for Santa Claus. The firefighters and local police officers who are on duty attend Christmas Eve mass at church—if there are no fires or emergencies, of course.

When the firefighters' shift ends on Christmas day, they go home and open presents with their families.

"It's a different way to spend the holidays," Chief Martinez says. "But it's still special. After all, my fellow firefighters are like my second family."

"Wow," says Lincoln. "Thank you for all you do!"

"It's my pleasure," says Chief Martinez.

Just then, the parade starts. Lincoln and Sam cheer as the floats and marching bands pass by. But they cheer loudest for Engine 19.

The next morning, Lincoln helps his mom bake Christmas cookies. Then they pack up the cookies and head over to Station 17. When they pull up in front, Sam squeals with delight.

Next to the station's entrance, a sign with big painted letters reads, "WINNER OF THE FIRE STATION CHRISTMAS DECORATION CONTEST."

"I knew they would win!" Lincoln shouts. "The dogs and cats at the shelter will be so happy!"

Lincoln and his parents go inside to deliver the cookies. The firefighters gather around them for a taste.

"Thank you so much for thinking of us!" Chief Martinez says.

"And thank you for keeping the community safe on Christmas Eve!" says Lincoln.

That night, the firefighters of Station 17 nestle all snug in their bunks. It's been another great Christmas season at the fire station.

Printed in the USA
CPSIA information can be obtained
at www.ICGtesting.com
CBRC091748301124
18173CB00017BA/130